To my beautiful and courageous daughter Aubrielle E. Jackson.

I have been blessed beyond measure the day I met you and started our journey together.

Introduce the suggested list of vocabulary words with students. Before reading, this book to students introduce vocabulary so that students may deepen their understanding relating to Type One Diabetes.

FOR K-2ND GRADE THIS BOOK CAN BE USED AS A READ ALOUD.

Vocabulary!!! As teachers read to students, introduce at least 2-3 words with students each day. Stop at different points of the story and ask questions. Make sure children fully understand this concept.

Teachers may use their creativity to create any activities for students to gain knowledge of Type One Diabetes vocabulary.

FOR THIRD-FIFTH OPTIONS FOR THIS BOOK.

Students should locate all vocabulary words while reading and discuss vocabulary while in small group. After small group, students can choose from any of the activities from the menu below.

Use five vocabulary words to complete five detailed sentences. Sentences must contain a noun, verb, adjective, and an adverb.

Use five or more vocabulary words to write a paragraph related to Type One Diabetes. Each Paragraph must have at least five detailed sentences. * Refer to Menu item #1. As a reference for detailed sentences.

Use vocabulary words to create a poem. For Acrostic, poem students must use five vocabulary words to make five different Acrostic poems.

Use each vocabulary word to make a crossword puzzle. Crossword puzzles must have detailed clues. (Hint)

Use the glossary provided.

Use vocabulary words to create a comic. Each comic should have pictures and onomatopoeias or complete sentences.

Hello, my name is Aubrielle or Aubrie for short. I was only 4 years old doing typical things any other kid my age would love to do, like eating ice cream, riding my bike, and having sleepovers.

Then, one day my whole life changed!

This was not something that happened to me all of a sudden. My mom and dad noticed I was acting different. They both noticed that I had become very thirsty FREQUENTLY. I was often tired, and started to lose a lot of weight.
My parents took me to visit my PEDIATRICIAN right away to see if there was a problem.

After seeing my pediatrician he told my parents I needed to go to the hospital right away! I took a deep breath and had a strange feeling in my throat as if I wanted to cry but I could not. So many questions raced through my mind. Once we arrived at the hospital, my eyes raced around the building, curious about what would happen next. Once inside the doctors ran so many tests to see what was wrong with me. After waiting for a while, the doctor walked in and said to my mom and dad "your daughter has type one diabetes." My mom grabbed my hand and **assured** me I would be just fine.

I was immediately assigned a whole team of doctors and nurses. They all made me feel very comfortable during my stay at the hospital.

I instantly started to feel much better after just one night.

I MET SOME REALLY SPECIAL PEOPLE WHO WERE JUST LIKE ME. THEY ALSO HAD TYPE ONE DIABETES. DR. DAN WAS THE COOLEST OF THEM ALL! DR. DAN SHOWED ME HOW MY GLUCOSE MONITOR WOULD WORK. HE HAD ONE HIMSELF! WHO KNEW THAT MY DOCTOR WOULD HAVE TYPE ONE DIABETES JUST LIKE ME? I MEAN HE LOOKED PERFECTLY FINE AND HEALTHY. IT WAS RIGHT THEN AT THAT MOMENT THAT I KNEW, I WOULD BE JUST FINE TOO!

The most important information the doctors showed me was how my GLUCOSE MONITOR would work. My glucose monitor makes sure that my glucose levels are not too high or too low. The coolest part about my glucose monitor is that it makes music sounds to let me know if I will need insulin or not. Insulin is very important when dealing with type one diabetes. Insulin makes sure my body has energy to do all the fun things I love to do.

We stayed at the hospital for four days. My parents and I learned so much information to care for me before returning home.

We learned about counting my carbs, insulin, and even the amount of exercise a person my age needed daily.

During my stay at the hospital my mom stayed with me every night. I love sleeping next to my mom she gives me a sense of comfort. We watched movies together all night. Watching movies with my mom made me feel better. My dad worked very hard with all of the doctors. My dad learned a lot from all of the doctors especially the DIETICIAN because my dad and I love to eat, especially together!

Finally, it was time to go home! I was feeling like my old self again. The road ahead would be long and challenging, but the doctors and nurses had given us enough information and RESOURCES to help us at every step of the way. My parents and I were excited to go home after a long four days in the hospital.

Now today a year later I live a normal life. I still do all of the activities I did before I was diagnosed with type one diabetes. I still eat ice cream, ride my bike, and have sleepovers. The only difference is I make sure I eat healthy portions of food, and enjoy good amounts of physical activity every day.

So if you and your parents ever find yourselves dealing with type one diabetes you are not alone. Nearly 13,000 children are diagnosed each year in America alone. I live a normal life just like any other kid my age. I have learned to be very brave so I can live a long and healthy life. I want each child that may be dealing with type one diabetes to know they are not alone and

DO NOT BE AFRAID!

GLOSSARY

DIABETES - Sometimes called sugar diabetes is a condition that occurs when the body can't use glucose (a type of sugar) normally.

GLUCOSE - the main source of energy for the body's cells.

FREQUENTLY - The condition of something happening or occurring over and over again.

PEDIATRICIAN - A doctor who takes care of babies, kids, and teens.

ASSURED - Characterized by certainty or security.

INSTANTLY - Happening or coming immediately.

GLUCOSE MONITOR - A small, portable machine that is used to measure how much glucose (a type of sugar) is in the blood (also known as the blood glucose level)

WARNING SIGNS TO LOOK FOR IN KIDS WHO MIGHT HAVE TYPE ONE DIABETES:

- INCREASED THIRST AND FREQUENT URINATION. EXCESS SUGAR BUILDING UP IN YOUR CHILD'S BLOODSTREAM PULLS FLUID FROM TISSUES

- EXTREME HUNGER

- WEIGHT LOSS

- FATIGUE

- IRRITABILITY OR BEHAVIOR CHANGES

- FRUITY-SMELLING BREATH

- BLURRED VISION

- YEAST INFECTION IN GIRLS

Made in the USA
Coppell, TX
01 December 2019